Whale

David Holman has an 'international reputation for young people's work with adult impact and quality'. *Guardian*

The story of Putu, Siku and K'nik, the three Grey whales trapped beneath the ice of North Alaska, caught the imagination and sympathy of the world, bringing together American, Russian and Inuit in the rescue operation.

Specially written for 7-12 year olds and family audiences, **Whale** opened at the National Theatre, London on 12 December 1989.

The play is rich in possibilities for discussion of Green issues, Russian-American relations, Inuit culture and the impact of media coverage for this and similar events. The National Theatre has created a background teaching pack to accompany the production.

David Holman's previous work includes **The Small Poppies**: 'Genuinely touching for all age groups.' (*City Limits*) and **No Worries**: 'Audiences were spell bound. Scarcely a dry eye in the house.' (*Time Out*)

David Holman has written more than 70 works for stage, radio, film and opera which have been performed for or by children. His work has been translated into many languages and been produced on every continent. Many of these works have explored environmental questions. These include his most performed play **Drink the Mercury** (1972) about the effects of heavy metal pollution on the fishermen of Minamata in Japan. **Adventure in the Deep** (1973) whose subject is the despoilation of the oceans. **Big Cat, Big Coat** (1980) and **Solomon and the Big Cat** (1987) which concern endangered species in Africa, and his most recent play, **Operation Holy Mountain** (1989) on the second coming of the patron Saint of animals, Francis of Assissi. Other widely performed plays are **No Pasaran** (1976) **The Disappeared** (1979), **Peacemaker** (1980), **No Worries** (1984) and **The Small Poppies** (1986).

Playstage: six plays for primary schools
six one-act plays for performance in class by 6-9 year-olds. Written by Andrew Davies, David Wood and Steven Eales and edited by John Alcock

The Business of Good Government
a nativity play by John Arden and Margaretta D'Arcy with production notes on costumes, properties and the singing of the music

Sweetie Pie
a play about women in society devised by Bolton Octagon Theatre-in-Education Company, edited and introduced by Eileen Murphy for 14 year-olds upwards

It's a Girl!
by John Burrows, a play with a capella music on the issues of childbirth and nuclear waste

Skungpoomery
a play by Ken Campbell originally written for the Nottingham Playhouse Roundabout Company for 7-13 year-olds

Timesneeze
a participatory play by David Campton originally written for the Young Vic for 7-11 year-olds

The Incredible Vanishing!
a play by Denise Coffey originally written for the Young Vic for 8-12 year-olds

The Adventures of Awful Knawful
a play by Peter Flannery and Mick Ford originally written for the RSC Kids' Show for 7-11 year-olds

One Cool Cat
a play by John Laing winner of the 1983 Play for Polka Competition for 6-10 year-olds

Pongo Plays 1-6
six short plays by Henry Livings with music by Alex Glasgow for 12 year-olds upwards

Six More Pongo Plays
six short plays by Henry Livings with music by Alex Glasgow for 12 year-olds upwards

Animal Farm
a dramatisation of George Orwell's satirical novel by Peter Hall, with music by Richard Peaslee and lyrics by Adrian Mitchell

Six Theatre-in-Education Programmes
six programmes, edited by Christine Redington

Theatre-in-Education Programmes: Infants
edited by Pam Schweitzer, five programmes for 5-8 year-olds

Theatre-in-Education Programmes: Secondary
edited by Pam Schweitzer, four programmes for 12 year-olds upwards

Live Theatre
four plays for young people by C.P.Taylor originally staged by the Tyneside Touring Live Theatre Co.

The Secret Diary of Adrian Mole 13³/4 – The Play
by Sue Townsend

Theatre Box
five plays for 8-12 year-olds from the Thames Television Theatre Box series. They have been adapted by Jonathan Dudley so that they can be staged by or for children, and with the minimum of apparatus or as lavishly as funds permit

Marmalade Atkins
by Andrew Davies

Death Angel
by Brian Glover

Reasons to be Cheerful
by James Andrew Hall

You Must Believe All This
by Adrian Mitchell

The Prince and the Demons
by George Moore

Whale

The story of
Putu, Siku and K'nik

A family audience play
for a multi-racial cast

David Holman

Methuen Drama

Methuen Young Drama

First published in Great Britain by Methuen Drama,
Michelin House, 81 Fulham Road, London SW3 6RB
and distributed in the United States of America by HEB Inc,
70 Court Street, Portsmouth, New Hampshire 03801.

Whale *copyright © 1989, David Holman*

A CIP catalogue record for this book is available from the British Library.

ISBN 0-413-63090-0

Printed in Great Britain by Cox & Wyman Ltd, Reading

The image on the front cover is by Michael Mayhew and Rose Towler
(from Associated Press photographs) © Royal National Theatre.

Author's Preface

I was already writing this play about the North Alaska grey whale rescue when news came that the shores of Prince William Sound in Southern Alaska had been devastated by one of the worst oil spills in history. The supertanker *Exxon Valdez* had gone aground and hundreds of thousands of birds, fish and mammals, including whales, were going to die.

Earlier I had met the National Theatre's Artistic Director, Richard Eyre to talk about plays for children and he was looking for a new work that was 'celebratory'. This prompted me to suggest a play based on the story of Siku and Putu and **K'nik, the** Grey whales you may remember as Crossbeak, Bonnet and Bone. I had been very impressed by the world-wide concern of children in their rescue and a big theatre offered the chance of producing a large scale work that could pay proper tribute to that concern.

When the details and pictures came in of what damage and death was being done in Prince William Sound, any sense of celebration for Alaska just vanished. In the course of a few months the small victory of the rescue of two whales was now being overwhelmed by the giant ecological defeat of a major oil spill. And my half-finished 'celebratory' play had become a kind of lie.

The reason **Whale** did get finished is, I suppose, the tremendous interest and concern for Putu, Siku and K'nik among children I continued to meet, a concern that symbolised something that spread much further than the ice of North Alaska – to the whole fate of this planet. The whale rescue had given these children hope that we might, before it is too late, learn a different way of seeing this planet. It may be a very slim chance – Exxon among many others were making it slimmer by the day – but it is a chance and perhaps that is worth celebrating with all its ironies. Perhaps such optimism is best expressed in this prophecy of a Canadian Indian from the Kwakkuitl tribe of British Columbia:

> When the Earth has been ravaged and the animals are dying, a tribe of people from all races, creeds and colours will put their faith in deeds, not words, to make the land green again. They will be called 'Warriors of the Rainbow', protectors of the Environment.

If this Indian is right I think he must be talking about you and your generation. So to all young 'Warriors of the Rainbow' – best wishes and I hope very much that you find something to enjoy in this play.

To the memory of Fernando Pereira of the *Rainbow Warrior*. Killed in Auckland Dock, New Zealand, 10 July 1985

Characters

Putu *a Grey whale*
Siku *a Grey whale*
K'nik *a baby Grey*
Storyteller
The Raven
Sedna *The Inuit Spirit of the Sea*
Old Inuit Man
Old Inuit Woman
Other Inuit
Inuit Lover 1
Inuit Lover 2
Arctic Fish
Seals
Sea Lions
Elephant Seals
Walruses
Bowhead and Grey Whales
Dennis the Whaler
Young Bill, *son of Dennis*
Joe the Whaler
Polar Bears
Mary Lou McKay *Disc Jockey*
Steve *her Producer*
Mrs Sandoval *Wife of Alaskan Oil Executive*
Mrs Kaiser *a keen golfer*
Sal the Golfer
Teddy the Golfer
Bob *a young Alaskan Oil Executive*
Charles *a young Alaskan Oil Executive*
Caddy 1
Caddy 2
National Guard General *(voice only)*
National Guard Sergeant
National Guard Corporal
Minneapolis Dad
Mum *his wife*
Candy *his daughter*
Minneapolis Kids
Mrs Soderstrom *a Marina Owner*

Soviet Sailors
Arctic Birds
Soviet Ship Captain
Soviet Second Officer
Ricky *American Whale Rescuer*
Press Photographer
Australian Journalist
Modern Inuit Kids
Old Inuit *Joe's Grandma*
San Francisco Cemetery Guide
Tourists
Spirit of Charles Scammon
a nineteenth century Whaling Captain

Whale was premièred at the Lyttelton Theatre on 12 December 1989 with the following cast:

Peter Caffrey, George Costigan, Basil Isaac, Paterson Joseph, Suzette Llewellyn, Toshie Ogura, Garrett Pennery, Dev Sagoo, Maggie Steed, June Watson, Toyah Willcox, Emil Wolk

Director Tim Supple
Designer Ashley Martin Davies
Lighting Mark Henderson
Music Peter Salem
Choreographer Melly Still

Note
Where shown, characters speak in Inuktitut, the language of the Inuit (Eskimo) or in Russian. Sedna speaks in Inuktitut throughout. The English translation is shown in brackets. Thanks to Hugh Brody for the Inuktitut translation and to William Powell for the Russian.

Act One

Scene One

With strong Inuit drum accompaniment the **Storyteller** *comes forward. Drumming breaks up the introduction.*

Storyteller Tavvauvussi surusit. (Greetings to you young ones.) Greetings young ones from the people of the northern ice. Home of the seal, home of the white bear, home of the whale.

From the very ancient times we have lived together with the whale. We cannot live without the whale, the whale cannot live without us. We are the people of the whale.

But we know that, one morning, we may go down to the edge of the ice and no longer hear the call of the whale because the great ships have killed them all. That is why we bring our story. So that the whale which is in our hearts will live also in yours.

It is a story that begins before there were whales in the sea, before there were seals, before arctic fish swam, before the first white bear prowled the ice floes.

Lights come up on the igloo.

Storyteller When all the world was empty except for an old man and old woman.

The two Inuit appear. An **Old Man** *and an* **Old Woman***. They are lightly singing a song in Inuktitut.*

Sunavinuk?
Arvingunavuguk?
Vugungnai?
ai ai ai ai
Arvingudlunu
Pinasuartaulaarpugungai?
ai . . . ai . . . ai . . . ai.

(What shall we be?
Shall we be whales?
Shall we?
ai ai ai ai
Being whales
We will be hunted, won't we?
ai . . . ai . . . ai . . . ai.)

Storyteller (*over song*) They lived all alone on a small island of ice in the middle of the icy sea.

The **Old Woman** *takes a vessel from the igloo and comes slowly forward to the edge of the stage.*

Storyteller One day the old woman came down to the sea to get water.

The **Old Woman** *lies down on the ice while the* **Old Man** *goes on singing and working.*

Storyteller Not seeing that across the sea was floating towards her – a feather. A black, black feather. And the feather floated right into her mouth.

Old Woman Aghhhhhhhhhhhhhhhhhhhhh.

The **Old Man** *stops singing and looks at her as she runs back to him. Holding her stomach.*

Old Woman Ajjigingititausimavunga! (Look what's happened to me!)

As the **Old Woman** *tells the* **Old Man** *what has happened to her the* **Storyteller** *continues.*

Storyteller Time passed and the old woman's stomach grew bigger and bigger and one day she gave birth – to a raven.

The baby **Raven** *is born.*

Raven Caaaaaaaaaaaaaaaaaaaaaaaawwwwwwwwwwwwwww.

The **Raven** *is a lively, mischievous but slightly funny figure. He caws continuously. The parents try to get it down and baby it. There is a moment of calm and they cuddle the* **Raven**.

Both Inuit Ohhhhhhhhhhhhhhhhhhhhhhh. Unakuluk

Storyteller The man and woman loved their baby but it was the most mischievous child that ever came into the world.

Raven Cawwwwwwwwwwwwwwwwwwwwwwwwww

Storyteller Sometimes they were in despair.

Raven Cawwwwwwwwwwwwwwwww.

Storyteller One day they had something to do and they shut their baby up for a few moments in their house of ice.

They shut the **Raven** *into the house.*

Raven Cawwwwwwwwwwwwwwwwwwww.

Old Man Tigusingilaurit nukapiak. (Don't touch anything.)

Storyteller And please don't you dare touch anything, youngster. And especially don't touch the bladder. Back soon. Rub noses.

The **Raven** *calms and makes to cry.*

Both Inuit Ohhhhhhhhhhhhh.

They leave, supporting each other, so tired with the baby **Raven***.*

Raven Caaaaaaawwwwwwwwwwwwwwwwww.

Storyteller Since the beginning of time a large bladder had hung from the ceiling. The couple didn't know what was in it but they knew it should never be touched.

Raven Caaaaaaawwwwwwwwwwwwwwwwww.

And the igloo turns round to show the **Raven** *and the bladder. He is pecking at everything on ground level. Then he looks up and sees the bladder. Looks interested.*

Raven Caaawwwwwwwwwww.

He starts to look like he might peck at it.

Storyteller Until that moment all the world had been dark. Though nobody knew it, it was because all the light in the world was locked up for safety in the bladder. No, Raven!!!

The **Raven** *pecks at the bladder. Brightest lights on the stage. Big music dissonance.* **Raven** *looks very confused.*

Raven Caaaaaaaaawwwwwwwwwwwww.

Both Inuit (*rushing on*) Aghhhhhhhhhhhhhhhhhh

Raven Caaaaaaaaaaaawwwwwwwwwwwwwww!!!!!!!!!!!!!

Storyteller Suddenly the whole world was flooded with light. The old man and the old woman rushed to stop all the precious light escaping.

They do so. The **Raven** *still screaming and looking sorry for himself. The* **Old Woman** *closes the bladder while the* **Old Man** *beats the* **Raven** *on the bottom. He howls.*

Old Man Irnikulualuga! (Look what you've done my child!)

Storyteller Half the light had escaped before the old woman could close the bladder. And that is why, from that moment, the world has had both day – and night.

Back to the original lighting.

Old Man Tulugagulualuk! (You naughty raven!)

Old Woman Aksualuk aniqujaudlutigit ikumak. (You've let out so much light.)

They shake their heads and leave. The **Raven** *starts to cry again. Then calms.*

Storyteller The raven grew strong and handsome but naturally he wanted to put his beak into everything. He was so curious. He longed to find out if there was anyone else in the world besides his Mother and Father. So one day he flew away.

The **Raven** *flies.*

Storyteller Mile after mile across the snow and the ice. Until –

Music.

A group of Inuit enter with an umiak, (boat). All the following should have an element of dance in the movement. Nose to nose singing in Inuktitut. Leaving the boat they start playing an Inuit game. A giant cat's cradle.

The **Raven** *lands some way away from the Inuit.*

Raven Mmmmmmmmmmmmmmmm.

Inuit Qiuvit? Qiuvit?
Unaktumingai ai
ai iai iai iai . . . aii iai iai
Nirijaktuvugungai ai ai ai
ai ai . . . aiangai . . . ai iai

(Are you cold? Are you cold?
On hot soup eh?
ai iai iai iai . . . aii iai iai
We can feast together, can't we?
ai ai . . . aiangai . . . ai . . iai)

The **Raven** *watches them with great interest and copies their game privately with his claws.*

The **Raven** *comes towards them shyly and signs to them he would like to join in their game.*

Raven Caaaaaaaaaawwwwwwwwwwww.

They see him. Stop for a moment. Then turn away. They are very wary of him and perhaps frightened.

Raven Aghhhhhhhhhhhhh.

Disappointed he continues to watch them.

Two of the young men are particularly fond of one young girl called **Sedna**. **Sedna** *is having her beautiful hair combed by her mother. The two young men are courting* **Sedna**. *She detaches herself coquettishly from her mother. The young men have become a bit too forward. This brings her nearer to the* **Raven**.

Storyteller The girl with the most beautiful hair was called Sedna.

The **Raven** *is very impressed. He falls in love with* **Sedna**.

Raven Ohhhhhhhhhh.

One of the young males comes over and signals to **Sedna** *that he wants to marry her. She shakes her head. He returns to the group. Some laughter. Then the other young man presents himself. He offers to marry her too.* **Sedna** *shakes her head.*

The **Raven** *is pleased. It occurs to him that* **Sedna** *might accept him. He spruces himself up. Shakes up the feathers on his head. Then strides across the stage. He presents himself to the young* **Sedna**.

Raven Caw. Caw. Caw. Caw.

Sedna *looks around herself nervous. She laughs and looks as if she wants some time to think. The* **Raven** *looks happy with this.*

Sedna *goes back to the group and explains what has happened to the two young men who have courted her. They nervously come over to the* **Raven**. *They whisper and sign to the* **Raven** *that he will have an answer in a moment. This is to give them time to make their escape as they fear him now.*

The **Raven** *looks satisfied. And he goes a few paces off. He ruffles up his feathers again. He is in good spirits. He is now not looking at them.*

The two young men carefully and slowly help **Sedna** *into the boat. Then swiftly and cautiously all the Inuit lift the boat and flee from the* **Raven** *to music.*

The **Raven** *continues to ruffle his feathers and preen. Then he looks round for her answer. He sees there is no one there. Looks all around. Lets out a giant and disappointed sound. He is very upset and hurt.*

Raven Caaaaaaaaaaaaaaaawwwwwwwwwwwwwwww!!!!!!!!!!!!!!

He does a small sad reprise of the cat's cradle game. He would perhaps have accepted just to play with someone. But he then determines to do something. The **Raven** *flies off and out as music tempo increases.*

The two **Lovers** *and* **Sedna** *enter with the umiak. The* **Lovers** *place* **Sedna** *in the umiak and then jump in themselves. They take out the paddles and paddle furiously.*

Both Young Inuit Uimak! Uimak! (Faster! Faster!)

After a while they paddle less rigorously. They have been looking back continuously. Now they feel they are safe. The two young men clasp each other.

Then a giant **Raven** *croak.*

Raven (*off*) Caaaaaaaaaaaawwwwwwwwwwwwwwwwwwwwwwwwwww.

We should understand this to be the cry of a disappointed **Raven** *rather than a homicidal one. But to the Inuit it sounds terrifying.*

A giant shadow of the **Raven** *appears behind them.*

With a cry of terror, they pick up their paddles and start paddling furiously again. But the sounds of the chasing and disappointed **Raven** *get louder. Inuit are shouting at each other, scared that the* **Raven** *is going to catch them.*

Both Young Inuit Uimak! Uimak! (Faster! Faster!)

Then they turn and look at **Sedna**. *(It being she not they the* **Raven** *chases.)*

Both Young Inuit Sedna!!!

Terrified, they grab hold of her to throw her overboard. **Sedna** *screams at them.*

Sedna Taimangillusi! (Please don't do it!)

They grasp her more strongly and force her out of the boat. They grab for their paddles. **Sedna** *turns and swims to the boat. The* **Lovers** *are trying to get the umiak moving.*

Storyteller Perhaps they could escape if the Raven saw Sedna drowning.

Sedna *grabs for the boat's side.*

Raven (*off*) Caaawwwwwwwwwwwwwwwwwwwwwww.

They bring their paddles down on her hands. She screams but still holds on.

Raven (*off*) Caaaaaaaaaaaaaaaaawwwwwwwwwwww!!!!!!!

Storyteller But Sedna she held on. The young men took their knives and slashed down.

Both Young Inuit Tuqusiliravit! (Die Sedna!)

Sedna Aghhhhhhhhhhhhhhhhhhhhhhhh.

Storyteller And Sedna's bloody fingertips fell into the icy water.

Dancers *enter and dance in fish-like movement round the umiak.*

Storyteller Sedna's fingertips spiralled deep deep below the surface of the icy water. And slowly they began to turn into the first fishes in the world. But still Sedna held on.

Raven (*off*) Caaaaaaaaaawwwwwwwwwwwwwwwwwwww.

The **Lovers** *look back behind them and raise their knives again.*

Both Young Inuit Tuqutaujuksauvutit uvattinut! (We must kill you Sedna!)

And they plunge the knives downwards again.

Sedna Aghhhhhhhhhhhhhhhhhhhhhh.

Storyteller And now the bloody second joints of Sedna's fingers fell into the water.

Other dancers enter (or previous dancers, if necessary) and dance round the boat as the seals and sea lions.

Storyteller And slowly slowly these turned into the seals and sea lions of the Arctic seas. But still Sedna hung on to the umiak with what was left of her bloody hands.

Raven (*off*) Caaaaaaaaaaaaaaawwwwwwwwwwwwwwwwwwww!!!!

Both Young Inuit Tuqutaujuksauvutit uvattinut. (You must die Sedna.)

And they slash down with their knives again.

Sedna Aghhhhhhhhhhhhhhhhhhhhhh.

Storyteller And the bottom joints of Sedna's fingers fell into the sea.

Dancers enter (or previous dancers, if necessary), as elephant seals and walruses.

Storyteller And these fingers turned into the elephant seals and the walruses. Now only Sedna's thumb held her to the umiak.

The **Lovers** *slash down again.*

Sedna Aghhhhhhhhhhhhhhhhhhhhh.

Dancers (or previous dancers), enter to be the whales.

Storyteller And Sedna's thumb fell deeper than any finger, down and still down to the bottom of the ocean and there turned into the whales of the Arctic, the Bowhead and the Grey.

And **Sedna** *releases her hands from the boat and, as if drowning, joins up with the dancers.*

Storyteller And Sedna too dropped deep into the ocean where she lives to this day. Sometimes she forgets that the humans caused her injuries and allows the fish and seals and whales to swim to the Inuit to become their food. But sometimes Sedna is so unhappy that she neglects her beautiful hair so that it becomes matted and ugly. And then the seals and whales get caught in her hair and they drown.

During this the dancers have taken **Sedna** *out.*

Slowly and cautiously some Inuit enter and come towards the umiak.

Storyteller The umiak was found but the storm that Sedna had caused in cursing the Raven had drowned the two young men. The Inuit found only long streaks of blood on one side and the clawings of finger nails.

The Inuit are worried by what they have found. They pick up the umiak and begin to exit.

The first sound of the whale. They look out to sea. Amazed.

An Inuit Qanuruna nipilik? (What is that sound?)

Storyteller But looking out to sea they saw first the raven crying for the loss of Sedna and promising some day to make good the harm he had done. Then – for the first time on earth the Inuit heard – the song of the whale.

The sound of the whale as Inuit exit chattering to each other.

Storyteller And today? The people of the Northern ice still hear the whale calling them.

Scene Two

Sound of whale call continues. On the ice. Howling wind. Amplified sound of a polar bear. Enter a polar bear. Roars continue.

Young Bill (*off*) Dad – you see that!!!

Dennis the Whaler (*off*) Shhh. If there's an injured whale under the ice the bear will show us where. She likes Bowhead meat as much as we do.

The polar bear starts to move off. A final roar. Then three battery lights appear. These are the hunters. Wind still howling.

Dennis the Whaler Follow me son. I can hear a Bowhead whale calling somewheres. No more junk food for you. Tonight we eat whale.

And two of them start to follow the polar bear.

Joe the Whaler *starts to move to the front of the stage with his light.* **Young Bill** *exits.* **Dennis the Whaler** *about to exit.*

Dennis the Whaler Joe?

Joe the Whaler Be a second.

Dennis the Whaler What is it? Bowhead?

Joe the Whaler Probably nothing. You go ahead.

Dennis the Whaler *leaves.* **Joe the Whaler** *moves another couple of paces forward.*

Joe the Whaler (*to himself*) Under the ice. Seal maybe.

Gets his rifle from his shoulder. Ready to fire. The sound of a whale spout. He jumps back.

Joe the Whaler Kid, you want to see a whale – there's three. It ain't the whale we want but – (*To the whales.*) You three should be halfway to Mexico by now.

Bill *re-enters.* **Dennis** *behind.*

Joe the Whaler Three Greys. They got caught in Sedna's hair and now they're trapped in the ice. Look like a baby, this one. Like a small snowflake.

Dennis the Whaler Still five tons of meat each. I'll get the harpoon.

Joe the Whaler They're Greys!!

Dennis the Whaler It'd feed the dogs.

Joe the Whaler It's not our whale. We're Bowhead Inuit.

Dennis the Whaler Joe, they're gonna die anyways. Hole's hardly big enough for them to breathe now and open sea's way too far for 'em to swim to it under the ice. (*To* **Young Bill.**) These need to breathe maybe every four minutes. From here they'd have to be underwater half an hour to get to open water. (*A beat. He considers their life expectancy.*) I give 'em coupla days maximum.

Young Bill Dad, this ice ain't that thick yet. Can't they –

Dennis the Whaler Greys ain't built to break ice son. That's why they head for Mexico September. October ice and these're finished. Drown. Bowhead – bang. Coupla feet thick ice no problem. Bowhead's got a head. Look there's already blood in the water. With little bitty thin ice to break.

Joe the Whaler Leave 'em to the polar bears. They smell that blood – aghhhhh. –

Dennis the Whaler OK. OK. Let's go find a real whale. I'm hungry.

Joe the Whaler Might tell that girl from Greenpeace 'bout these three.

Dennis the Whaler Yea, what's *she* gonna do? (*A great joke.*) Come out and break ice for them?

Dennis *and* **Young Bill** *think this is a tremendous joke.* **Joe** *joins in.*

Dennis the Whaler (*as he exits*) Yea. Unless Sedna starts combing her hair you three – Hey, call for the Raven. They say he helps hard luck cases.

And the wind comes up and they slowly exit still laughing.

Scene Three

Abrupt and loud entry of music. Freddie Ford's Sea Cruise.

The **Raven** *enters curious.*

Music continues through the following. Rapid.

Disc Jockey Station WXCL in Barrow, Alaska where it's 15 below and falling. This is rockin' Mary Lou McKay and *The Midnight*

Hour. Good moooooorrrrnnning Alaska!!!!! Seen that movie?
Freddie Ford's *Sea Cruise*. Playin this for you 'cause with the heavy
early ice we got up here on the North coast of Alaska this year
ain't nobody going on no sea cruise less it's on an icebreaker. *The
Midnight Hour*. I'll have local news momentarily – after this
message.

The **Raven** *is listening and watching.*

*Into an ad. for local goods. She turns this down. She looks at a single sheet
of paper, very annoyed.*

Disc Jockey (*flicking switch*) Mr Producer Man. Stevie?? Yeah, you
behind the glass. What is this??

Radio Producer (*off*) That's your local news Mary Lou.

Disc Jockey Steve?

Radio Producer (*off*) It's a slow night.

Disc Jockey Listen when you're the furthest North Disc Jockey in
the world you don't expect big news but three iced-in whales??

The **Raven** *pricks up his ears.*

Disc Jockey Didn't nobody get drunk in town tonight? Crash a
snowmobile? Wasn't nobody born???

Radio Producer (*off*) Hey. Hey. My own kids gave me that story.
They ran into Joe the Whaler in town.

Disc Jockey So let *them* do the show. Whales get trapped all the
time.

Radio Producer (*off*) Not where you can see 'em struggling for
air from your window!!

Disc Jockey Steve – real news. I ain't reading this. (*Screws up whale
news paper and throws it behind her as the ad. finishes.*) Little delay on
the local news here. Meanwhile –

The **Raven** *moves to pick up the discarded paper. And the new record
starts as* **Producer** *comes in with some different papers.*

Radio Producer OK!!!! Coupla accidents.

Disc Jockey Be-bop-a-lula

Radio Producer Drunk drivers.

Disc Jockey Tutti-frutti.

Raven *excited at what he is reading.*

Radio Producer Fish prices.

Disc Jockey Da-doo-RUN-RUN!!!

Radio Producer Hey come on Mary Lou! I promised my kids.

Disc Jockey Steve, this is rock'n'roll talk radio. I got ten phones here. I want news that's going to get them reelin' and a ringin'. Iced-in whales. Forget it!

The **Producer** *goes and* **Disc Jockey** *flicks through pages and then places papers on her console.*

Disc Jockey (*interrupting record which still plays*) Local news coming right up.

She goes on listening to the music as the **Raven** *finishes what he is reading.* **Raven** *goes over to the console as* **Mary Lou** *is preoccupied with setting up a jingle.* **Raven** *takes the traffic reports etc. and slowly screws up each of them and throws them away or eats them.* **Disc Jockey** *busy and oblivious. The record finishes.*

Disc Jockey And now news from the North Slope tonight.

Jingle. She reaches down for the papers.

Disc Jockey Ugh?? (*Looks other side of her.*) Ugh?

The **Raven** *places the whale story in her hand.*

Jingle finishes. She looks at the paper she has.

Disc Jockey Ugh?

She looks around in panic for the news report. This whale story is all she's got.

She makes the best of it.

Disc Jockey (*cupping mike for a second*) Steve!!!! I'll kill – (*Uncups as jingle finishes.*) Heck of a story right here in Point Barrow for you tonight. Coupla kids of my aquaintance brought it in. Didn't think I'd be interested but it touched my heart and I know it's going to touch yours too. Concerns three Grey whales, yep, that's right, one of them no more than a baby, who should have left for the warm waters of Mexico days ago. Seems they've got a hole about thirty feet across they're breathing through but the ice is closing in fast. They're in bad shape. Kids I mentioned want to know if anyone has any ideas out there 'bout what we could do to help them. – on *The Midnight Hour.* Anyone? (*Cups mike.*) No one.

Immediate start to Beach Boys' Good Vibrations.

Raven Cawwwwwwwwwwwwwwwwwwwwwwwwwwww.

And **Raven** *dances around the stage.*

Disc Jockey, *mad as hell, rips off her cans.*

Disc Jockey Steve!!!! (*Pause.*) Steve!!! Get in here. Whales??
Listen I know how to get phones ringing. Ya hear that silence
Steve? Huh? Hear it? Steve I been getting phones ringing MY
WAY all my damn –

*Sound of phone ringing. Pause. Now two ringing. She hesitates. A third
ringing.*

Radio Producer (*off*) Mary Lou, lines one, two and three ringing.
(*A beat.*) Correction four and five.

Disc Jockey Calling 'bout what?

Radio Producer (*off*) Add six. Somethin 'bout whales Mary Lou.
Correction seven phones. Baby Grey whales.

Disc Jockey What?? (*Picks up phone.*) One second please.

Radio Producer *enters holding jacket.*

Radio Producer And eight. Suggestions 'bout how to help 'em,
Mary Lou. Remember? Little kids' story – touched your heart.

More ringing

Disc Jockey (*picking up second phone*) Whales? Sure. Anything you
want to say Sir? Oh Rosie? Age eight wants to – Right. Put her on,
Sir.

Radio Producer (*leaving*) Line nine.

Disc Jockey (*listening to two phones*) Uhuh. Uhuh. Right. Right.

Radio Producer Correction Mary Lou. Full house. Listen I think
I'm going for a cup of coffee while it's sooooo silent.

Disc Jockey You do and – !! (*To phone.*) No. Sorry.

Radio Producer (*putting on jacket*) Boney Maroney, Peggy Sue,
Mary Lou.

Disc Jockey Jerk!! (*To third phone.*) Not you Ma'am. Steve!!
Ma'am, could you give me a second. (*Another phone.*) Whales.
Sure. One second. (*Another phone.*) Yep. Whales. Excuse me.
Steve!! Steve!! (*Another phone.*) Excuse me. Right back. (*Shouts to*

Producer.) Steve, get those kids of yours in here.

Radio Producer (*exiting*) Coffee.

Disc Jockey Please. Please. Please. OK?

Producer *reappears. More ringing as the* **Raven** *dances.*

Disc Jockey (*to phone*) You think the Mayor should pay to keep the breathing holes open? (*Cups mike.*) Steve!! (*Uncups.*) You're six-years-old and you're listening to *The Midnight Hour*? Well that's a very interesting idea Scott. (*Cupping the mike.*) I don't believe this!! (*To* **Producer**.) I want your kids in here, Joe the Whaler, Greenpeace. Anyone. And now!! Please. (*As* **Producer** *takes off jacket and nods, she turns to new phone.*) Yes Ma'am. Do I like whales? Are you kidding?

Up Good Vibrations. *Mix in sharp burst of* **Raven**'s *laughter. Brief blackout continuing the* **Raven**'s *laughter. He is pretty pleased with his role.* **Raven** *noise stops.*

Scene Four

Music changes and into the light from the back of the stage painfully walks the sea goddess **Sedna**. *Her stumps of hands are bandaged and covered with blood. She makes an angry sound. Annoyed at the* **Raven**'s *interference. She is centre stage.*

Sedna) Puijungitiakpagit tulugak. (Oh no Raven. I haven't forgotten you.)

She gestures to call up the winds and the ice.

Sedna Anurit kailauritsi!!!! Siku kailaurit!!! (Come winds!!! Come ice!!!)

And the sounds of high Arctic winds. Ice straining and breaking. The radio voice mixes with the winds.

Radio Voice Station WKCJ Anchorage Alaska. Hopes for the three Grey whales are fading tonight.

Sedna *listens to the ice form.*

Radio Voice Night after night Inuit whalers have been keeping the breathing hole open, amazed at the public's interest coast to coast.

Sedna *raises her arms. More ice forms.*

Radio Voice But, as I speak, freezing winds are rapidly closing the breathing hole. The Inuit are cutting fast but the ice is freezing faster. They need a miracle in the next 24 hours and I mean a miracle.

Sedna *exits.*

Scene Five

Lights up on a golf course in Florida. A pin flag in the centre of the stage. The eighteenth hole. A young woman, **Mrs Sandoval**, *the wife of an Alaskan oilman, waits front stage. She is plenty mad. Golfers pass across backstage.* **Mrs Sandoval** *has a small airline bag over her shoulder. She has sunglasses on. Looking up the eighteenth fairway with her back to us. She waits, angry. A jaunty older woman golfer enters in tropical style gear with a driver in one hand and a ball and tee in the other.*

Mrs Kaiser (*to departing golfer*) Hi Teddy. Whatya shoot? (*To* **Mrs Sandoval**.) Morning.

Teddy 103.

Mrs Sandoval Morning.

They have never met before.

Mrs Kaiser (*to departing* **Teddy**) Attaboy Teddy. (*To* **Mrs Sandoval**.) Florida. Ahhh (*Talking while placing the tee for a practice swing. Away from the eighteenth.*) Sun and golf. Heaven.

Mrs Sandoval (*without interest and still looking up the fairway.*) Right.

Mrs Kaiser (*shouts*) Fore. (*She waits. Someone there. She tries a practice swing away from the ball.*) Those poor whales could do with some of this huh? Melt that ice. (*Shouts.*) Fore!! Oswaldo I'm trying to tee off here!! (*To* **Mrs Sandoval**.) I got three grandchildren won't leave the TV. Oswaldo! 'What's gonna happen to little K'nik Grandma?' I mean what are ya supposed to say?

And **Mrs Sandoval** *has burst into floods of tears. Surprised pause from* **Mrs Kaiser** *as the tears flow.*

Mrs Kaiser What's the matter honey? (*Slowly and tentatively leaving the ball and coming over to her.*) Honey, what the – I say something?

Still tears. **Mrs Sandoval** *shakes her head.* **Mrs Kaiser** *looks at* **Mrs Sandoval**'s *airline bag.*

Mrs Kaiser Alaska Oil Company. You on vacation from Alaska honey?

A nod with tears.

Mrs Kaiser What? You upset about those poor whales?

A nod and tears.

Mrs Kaiser You've seen them?

A nod and calming tears. A handkerchief is given.

Mrs Kaiser Blow. Don't worry about it. I got a million handkerchiefs. Hay fever. Had it all my – Again.

Mrs Sandoval Flying south pilot took the plane down real low over the ice so we could all – (*Another burst of tears.*)

Mrs Kaiser It's OK honey.

Mrs Sandoval I'm Pisces. I can't help it.

From the back a woman golfer enters across the eighteenth with her caddy carrying a golf bag. The caddy is the **Raven**.

Mrs Sandoval You could see their poor bloodsoaked heads crashing the ice just trying to get air. It isn't much to ask is it? Air?? But my husband won't help them get air.

Raven *has of course listened to this with great interest as he walks.*

Mrs Kaiser Hus –? (*To the Golfer.*) Hi Sal. Whatya shoot?

Sal Ninety-six.

Mrs Kaiser Attagirl. (*To* **Mrs Sandoval**.) Honey those Eskimos are doing all they can.

Mrs Sandoval (*pointing up the fairway*) But Alaska Oil could save those whales if . . . if!!!

A shiver of music. The **Raven** *stops.*

Mrs Sandoval I'm leaving him. My husband is a wimp!! Wimp!!

Mrs Kaiser Wait a – Alaska Oil? Your husband work for – ? (*Pointing up fairway.*) That him with the other guy?

The **Raven** *has tapped* **Sal** *on the shoulder. Gives her the golf bag. His caddy stint is over.* **Sal** *surprised.* **Raven** *pushes her roughly off stage.*

Mrs Sandoval Those two are sitting on equipment up there could break that ice. Their boss is away in Europe. I told Chuck – steal the stuff. Do something! 'Can't honey.' Everything by the book. They're not men they're yuppie mouses.

*The **Raven** stands close now listening attentively to the two women.*

Mrs Kaiser Mice. (*Beat.*) Sorry.

Charles (*off. From up the fairway*) Fore!!!!!

Mrs Sandoval I married a yuppie mice.

A golf ball arrives.

Mrs Sandoval A little mice.

Then another ball.

Mrs Sandoval (*indicating her husband's ball*) He plays golf when he could be – Poor little K'nik!! I'm packed. I'm leaving him.

Mrs Kaiser (*guiding **Mrs Sandoval***) You need a drink. Honey you can't blame your husband for not stealing valuable equipment. Probably worth thousands of dollars

Mrs Sandoval Millions. So what? (*Resisting being taken.*) No.

Mrs Kaiser Honey. Someone'll save those whales.

Mrs Sandoval (*pointing up fairway*) Only those two can save em. AND THEY WONT!!!!

*They exit while the **Raven** quickly comes to a decision. Voices are heard approaching.*

Raven Caaaaaaaaaawwwwwwwwwwww

*He looks up the fairway and then steals both balls. He puts them in his beak. He stands aside as **Bob** and **Charles**, the two golfers, enter carrying putters. Their caddies stand at the back silent. Both golfers look extremely puzzled not to see their golf balls.*

Bob (*looking around for his ball*) Wait a minute. Just wait a minute! I hit the green.

Charles Me too. I don't believe this. Hey hey. Know what's happened?

Bob Hole in one!! No.

*They rush to the hole with a tiny hope that they have miraculously holed out. **Bob** pulls out the pin. Cup is empty. They slump.*

Bob OK guys let's check the rough.

Caddies start checking back area of stage. The golfers front.

Charles I saw mine hit the green!!!

Bob (*demonstrating the empty green*)   Sure you did Chuck.

And they go to different sides of the stage and bend to search as in the long grass. The **Raven** *comes and whispers to* **Charles** *as all four search.*

Bob (*to the Caddies*)   Mine's a 'Curtis Strange' guys.

Raven *then stands and tip-toeing goes and puts the two balls in the hole. Golfers and caddies still searching.*

Charles Bob?

Bob What?

Charles Those whales.

Bob Chuck! Gimme a break.

Charles Idea.

Bob Your dumb wife's dumb idea and it's a no no. Goddamn grass!!

Charles What do they need?

Bob Where is my ball???

Charles A big crack in the ice.

Bob No.

Charles And what has Alaskan Oil got at Prudhoe Bay?

Bob It's no Chuck! One. That ice breaking barge? – you're talking grand larceny. You're talking Alcatraz.

Charles Not steal – borrow.

Bob Two. It's a million dollars worth of equipment. Three –

Charles They're gonna die.

Bob So they die. We'd be shining shoes.

Charles Boss wouldn't have to know.

Bob Whales die. It's nature Chuck. Don't interfere with nature.

Charles Inter – ? Nature made golf courses? That ice breaker could be with the whales in 24 hours which is all they've got Bob!!

Bob Four. You can't get the ice breaker to the whales anyways. Lost ball. What do you say? We'll never find these. We ain't got a 'copter big enough to drag it. Ya need a Sikorski.

They stop searching.

Charles Alaskan National Guard has a Sikorski. (*Using his club to demonstrate what will be planned.*) 'Copter hooks wires to the barge. Drags the barge to the whales and cracks 'em a path to the sea. Freedom!

Bob Yea? And you're gonna steal the chopper also? From the Army? You wouldn't see daylight this century. Any century. (*To caddies.*) OK guys, thanks. Lost ball. We're through. What did we say? 25 dollars each.

Bob *about to get out his wallet to pay the approaching Caddies.*

Charles Let's risk it.

Bob Chuck you never took a risk in your life. That's why you're earning a hundred grand a year. You're a yes man. It pays. Don't blow it for some dumb whales.

Raven *quickly whispers to* **Bob**.

Bob Hey. If I'd hit a hole in one I'd have done it with you. 'Kay? Steal the barge, then talk to the Army. I would. Word of honour.

Charles (*unimpressed*) Thanks.

Bob Let's go

They have both drifted back to the flag on the way out. **Raven** *nudges* **Charles** *towards the hole.* **Charles** *does a double take at the hole.*

Charles (*looking down into the hole. Hoarsely*) Bob?

Bob Gimme a break now.

Charles *beckons* **Bob**.

Bob Ugh?

Bob *a step towards hole.*

Bob (*looking down also*) Oh wow. Oh WOW!!!! (*Reaching down.*) I don't bel –.

Charles How could –

Bob (*with his ball*) My 'Curtis Strange'. Hole in one. (*He throws his *club into the air.*)

Pause.

Charles Bob. Just then. You say word of honour?

Bob Hey I didn't –

Charles You did.

Bob You got a witness? (*To the Caddies.*) There you are guys.
There's 25 each. And another 20. Bonus. (*To* **Charles**.) Don't
mean nothing without a witness buddy.

Charles Oh no. Bob. Oh Bob.

Pause.

First **Caddy** *hands back to* **Bob** *the bonus 20.*

Bob Hey, that's your bonus.

Caddy (*to* **Charles**) You need a witness buddy. You just got one.

Second **Caddy** *hands back his bonus 20.*

Caddy 2 You got two.

Bob Wait a minute. Wait a minute.

Caddy (*starts cracking his fingers*) Mac – you got stuff'll save them
whales and you gonna let 'em die – you can come right now and
explain that to my two kids. They been up all night for the TV
newsflashes.

Caddy 2 Then you come to my house and run it past big Louie.

Bob Big Lou – ?

Caddy Walk!

Bob Hey hey I was only joking guys. Uh? Uh? Chuck? Right? But
listen uh maybe there ain't a plane. Uh? I mean –

Caddy 2 My sister works at the Airport. She'll get ya' a plane.

Bob (*still nervous*) Great. Great. Well emmmmm. Yea. Right.
Right.

Mrs Sandoval *enters.*

Charles Honey.

Mrs Sandoval Chuck I've thought it over. I've called my lawyer
and it's D.I.V. –

Charles Can't talk now sweets. We've got whales to rescue.

Mrs Sandoval (*a beat*) What? What????? You're gonna –
Ohhhhhhh. Clark Kent lives! Ohhh.

*She throws herself into his arms. The **Raven** does a back somersault and
then flips into the arms of the Caddies.*

Raven Cawwwwwwwwwwwwwwwwwwwwwwwwwwwwwwwwwwwwww.

Blackout.

Scene Six

*Immediate sound of whirring helicopter above the stage. Snow is falling.
We see the wheels of the 'copter and two ropes coming down. Two strong
spotlights coming from the helicopter beaming down to two points several
feet apart on the stage. A person with back to the audience with the
coloured table tennis bats of the runway controller. An Alaskan **National
Guard Sergeant** in the spotlight is securing a rope which runs from the
helicopter above to the stage (as if stage is the icebreaking barge). Wears big
ear plugs. Towards back stage an Alaskan **National Guard Corporal**
with big ear plugs is doing the same with a second rope.*

National Guard Sergeant (*into walkie-talkie – shouting above 'copter
engine noise*) OK general the barge is secured to your underframe,
Sir. Problem is – this barge is so heavy if it's stuck to the ice
anywhere underneath even your Sikorski ain't going to shift it.
'Kay Sir.

*And the noise becomes deafening as the 'copter tries to get lift into the
barge. The snow swirls. The **National Guard Sergeant** waves arms as if
to help the 'copter lift. Great noise of metallic strain.*

National Guard Sergeant (*into walkie-talkie*) No General. No.
Throttle down. Too much!! Too much!!

*With a crack one of the ropes breaks. **National Guard NCOs** dive for the
floor. The other rope breaks. The 'copter sound lightens to a hum. The
Raven enters. Snow still swirling. **Raven** looks at the broken ropes and up
to the 'copter as the **National Guard NCOs** still have their hands over
their heads on the floor and are moaning. **Raven** jumps up and down in
frustration.*

National Guard Sergeant (*rising and into walkie-talkie*) Sir, we'll be
ready to try again in 24 hours. Less if the weather don't get any
worse. (*A beat.*) General? (*A beat.*) General?

The **National Guard Corporal** *is clearing the stage of the broken ropes etc.*

General (*off*) Soldier I'm just receiving a phone call.

National Guard Sergeant (*saluting*) Sir!

General (*off*) Know who's calling? Congratulating me on teaming up with the boys at Alaska Oil and asking me, soldier, at precisely what time the National Guard is going to get off its butt and be ready to start breaking ice for them there whales. Seems his TV screen at the White House (you gettin' the picture now son?) is telling him they got 16 hours maximum before their breathing holes freezes over. Now, soldier, maybe YOU want to come and tell the President of the US of A, you need 24 hours!!!

National Guard Sergeant (*into walkie-talkie*) Twelve Sir. Gimme twelve. Sir? Sir? Ten?

The sound of disconnected phone.

National Guard Sergeant Help!!!

And he exits shouting.

National Guard Sergeant Corporal get your ass in gear. We got whales to save and I mean now!!

Raven *gives a giant caw of frustration.*

Raven Caaaaaaaaaawwwwwwwwwwwwwwwwww!!

He gets down on his knees and bangs his head against the ice. A big electronic reverberation from his head hitting ice. The air-strip controller with the table tennis bats throws off her baseball cap. Loosens her hair. She turns. It is **Sedna**. *Lights fade as we hear the growing sound of the howling Arctic wind.*

Scene Seven

Suburban house. Minneapolis, Minnesota.

Kids, both boys and girls, enter rowdily in grid-iron football helmets in the colours of the Minnesota Vikings. One has the ball. They tackle and block. Screaming and shouting.

Kids Minnesota Vikings. Minnesota Vikings. Minnesota Vikings.

Candy, *daughter of the house, enters with portable TV.*

First Kid Game time guys.

Candy Who's gonna wup the New Orleans Saints? Gimme a 'V'.

Kids V.

Candy Gimme an 'I'.

Kids I.

Candy Gimme a 'K'.

Kids K.

Candy Gimme another 'I'.

Kids I.

Candy Gimme an 'N'.

Kids N.

Candy Gimme an 'G'.

Kids G.

Candy Gimme an 'S'.

Kids S.

Candy What have we got??

Kids VIKINGS. VIKINGS. VIKINGS.

Mum (*entering*) Quietttttt!!!!!!!

Some Kids Mommm!!!!

Mum Peace!!!

Total silence after bedlam.

Mum I'll say this I'll say it once. Your Dad's got a first customer for his ice breaking invention. Lady's just arrived. (*Silencing someone before they say a word.*) Uh! (*A beat.*) They'll want to talk in here. You want to watch the game in the lounge you do it with the sound off – Uh! (*A beat.*) Till the lady's gone. Don't even breathe loud. Uh! (*A beat.*) I do not put this to you for discussion. This is the way things will be. (*Turning with a big smile.*) Miss Soderstrom.

Dad *and customer enter.*

Minneapolis Dad (*kissing his wife*) Hi dear. (*Indicating for his wife to come forward to the window.*) Miss Soderstrom.

Kid (*whispering*) Boy, Candy, is your Mum always –

He freezes as he sees **Mum***'s look.*

They watch the screened ball game. Animated but silent.

Minneapolis Dad (*shouting outside*) OK Rick start her up so Miss Soderstrom can see how it works.

Miss Soderstrom Four hundred dollars right?

Minneapolis Dad And we deliver.

Miss Soderstrom Looks good. How many ya made?

Minneapolis Dad Just three. My partner and me are just starting.

The mechanical noise of a drill-like sound starts.

Minneapolis Dad OK as you see lake back of the house is frozen – five, six inches. You got a boat – can't use it. Can't fish, can't take trips. For just four hundred bucks and a can of gas you got ice-free water all winter.

Miss Soderstrom Hey. S'like an egg beater!! A big egg beater.

Minneapolis Dad Right.

Miss Soderstrom It's clearing that ice!!

Minneapolis Dad Why don't you step out and try if for yourself Miss Soderstrom. (*As* **Miss Soderstrom** *nods.*) Rick, Miss Soderstrom's comin' out. Show her the controls.

Miss Soderstrom If I like it I'm gonna need all three. I run a marina on Lake Superior.

Miss Soderstrom *exits.*

Mum *comes over to* **Dad***.*

Mum All three!!! Your first sale.

Minneapolis Dad Maybe.

Mum You've made a terrific ice melting machine. She's hooked.

And she kisses him and goes.

Minneapolis Dad (*to himself*) Come on. First sale. Kids, how's the game goin?

Candy We're down seven points.

Minneapolis Dad To New Orleans?

Candy They just broke into the game with news of the whales Dad.

The **Raven** *enters*

Minneapolis Dad (*still thinking of the sale*) Uhuh? How they doin'?

All the kids turn their thumbs down.

Minneapolis Dad Oh.

Raven *has a Minnesota Viking helmet under his arm and perhaps their shirt.*

He comes to sit with the kids.

Minneapolis Dad (*looking out of the window as* **Raven** *whispers to all the kids*) Atta girl Miss Soderstrom.Whip up that ice!!

Raven *is whispering to all the kids and pointing at the noise of the machine.* **Candy** *comes over from the TV and stands with* **Dad**.

Candy That's a great machine Dad.

Minneapolis Dad Thanks Candy. Half-time?

Candy (*shaking head*) Dad can I put one word in your ear?

Minneapolis Dad Candy I'm busy, OK? (*A beat.*) Sure.

Candy Whales Dad.

Minneapolis Dad Whales?

The kids at the TV all start looking at them.

Candy The Greys in Alaska, Dad. Army ain't managed to shift the barge out of Prudhoe. Inuit can't cut holes fast enough. They're gonna drown, Dad.

Other Kids That's right Sir.

First Kids It was on the news, Sir.

Candy Say they could be dead by tomorrow night Dad.

Minneapolis Dad Thought you kids were watching the Vikings!!

All Kids Yes Sir.

Candy If those Inuit guys had you and your machines Dad.

The Kids Right.

Minneapolis Dad (*fending it off*) Hey. Hey. Hey. Hey. Hey. OK?? (*Pause.*) Dead by tomorrow night? (*Silent nods.*) Hey. Hey. Hey. No. No Candy. What the – How'd me and Rick get to Alaska? What are you – Two round trip air-fares? You kiddin me? I –

The kids go immediately into their pockets for all the money they have.

Minneapolis Dad (*of their small change*) I mean – that'd get me to
the airport at Minneapolis. I'm still a thousand miles away. Think
I'm a millionaire or something? I'm a working Joe.

Kids look at him waiting, not accusing.

Minneapolis Dad Come on. Watch the game!

They turn to do so with one eye on him.

Pause.

Candy Dad the Christmas trip? How much you save if we all
didn't go?

Minneapolis Dad A grand. Maybe tw – I don't know. Hey!

Candy We want to skip that. Save the money. Right?

*She looks round the kids. All nod in turn though it hurts them a little. The
last one she looks at doesn't nod.*

Candy Rosie? (*A beat.*) Rosie?

Rosie *nods her head.*

Minneapolis Dad No. OK?

Another Kid Yes Sir.

They turn back to the game. **Dad** *looks at them. Kids half watch game.*

Minneapolis Dad You know how many hours me and Rick worked
this week? Seventy-one. Seventy-one hours. I don't need these
looks OK. OK? Some day I'd like to watch a ball game. Know what
I mean?? Car isn't near paid for. I got a gas bill I – boy. All I need
is – Kids! (*Quite a pause as he goes this way and that.*) Candy, move.
Grab my weekend bag. Quilted clothes. (**Candy** *runs.* **Dad** *moves
forward and shouts.*) Ricky – leave that. Get all the machines onto
the pickup. Miss Soderstrom – sorry Ma'am. Those machines ain't
for sale yet. Phone you next week. But if you want to see 'em
working thick ice watch National TV tomorrow. North Alaska. OK
kids let's go. We got a plane to catch.

They crowd round him as **Candy** *returns with bag.*

All Kids Yeaaaaaaa.

Candy Gimme a 'D'.

Kids D.

Candy Gimme an 'A'.

Kids A.

Candy Gimme another 'D'.

Kids D.

Candy And what have we got??

Kids (*as they carry him out*) Daaaaaaaaaaaaaaaaaaaad!!

Raven Cawwwwwwwwwwwwwwwwwwwwwwwwww.

Kids Dad! Dad! Dad! Dad!

They exit.

Raven *does a somersault and departs in a joyous dance.*

Scene Eight

North slope. Alaska.

Sound of the whales. Lights up. Sound of the whales cease. White stage with three separate air breathing holes. Sound of the strong wind. Snow falling. Music builds.

The three whales rising simultaneously, breach the water to breathe. One much smaller than the others. This is **K'nik.** *A rush of expelled air. They fill their lungs. They fall back into the water.*

Enter **Sedna**. *Bandaged hands. She stands over the hole of little* **K'nik**. *To music she holds her hands above her head. Winds come up. Whistles across the stage. The hole slowly starts to close. It closes.*

We hear the sound of the knocking under the ice. **Sedna** *looks down at the knocking and exits. Music builds again covering the sound.*

Joe *and another whaler,* **Dennis** *enter with* **Minneapolis Dad**. *He has one ice clearing machine. The Inuit have ice cutters.*

Joe the Whaler (*seeing the iced over hole*) K'nik!! (*To* **Minneapolis Dad**.) We're going to need your machine Mister. Now! K'nik!!

And all rush to the hole and start to crack at it with their ice cutters.

Joe the Whaler (*shouting above the wind*) Come on. Put your back into it. We've kept her alive for ten days. Can't let her go now. Come on. Do it for K'nik. Come on! Come on.

The hole slowly is made again. **Joe** *goes down on his knees at the hole.*

Joe the Whaler K'nik!!!! Quick, get your machine Mister.

Minneapolis Dad *places the ice twirling machine in the water. It starts to whirl.*

Joe the Whaler Good. Good. Great machine. We'll save her. K'nik! We'll save her. K'nik!

The music builds again as before.

We expect all three whales to breach now so positive have been the Inuit. And now all three holes are clear. The rushing sound of the whales about to breach. First **Putu** *breaches, breathes and falls back.*

Pause.

Then **Siku** *breaches, breathes and falls back.*

Everyone round **K'nik***'s ice hole. Hoping.*

Joe the Whaler K'nik. (*Pause.*) Come on K'nik!! (*Pause.*) Come on girl!! Come on!! K'nik!!! K'nik!!!!

Only the sound of the wind. **K'nik** *is dead.* **Dennis** *lets out a howl of frustration.*

Dennis the Whaler Sedna just won't let her go.

And throws down his ice cutter.

Joe the Whaler Tell you what I'm going to do. I'm going to harpoon these two.

Minneapolis Dad You're what? What??? Joe!! Who's kept them alive for ten days? You Inuit guys. Who cut ice all night every night? Harpoon them?

Joe the Whaler Mister, your machines are terrific. OK you can keep the holes open. Then what? Come here. What do you see out there?

Minneapolis Dad Ice. Just ice and then the sea.

Joe the Whaler Five miles of ice to the sea and more ice every minute. We been cutting new holes for these three to lead them towards the open sea. But the sea's icing up faster than we can get them to new holes. We need an icebreaker and there's no American ships closer than three hundred miles. Dennis I say we've done what we can. We harpoon 'em and eat them.

Dennis the Whaler *looks at the ice hole.*

Minneapolis Dad No.

A pause.

Dennis the Whaler I guess.

Minneapolis Dad Awwwwwwwwwwwwww.

As **Young Bill** *enters running, out of breath. He waits.*

Dennis the Whaler What's happening son?

Young Bill (*breathless*) Dad. You gotta keep the holes open another 24 hours.

Joe the Whaler Bill, we've done all we can do. It's finished.

Young Bill (*breathless*) Greenpeace been working round the clock trying to get an icebreaker here.

Joe the Whaler If there'd been one Greenpeace'd have found it. They got all the US shipping lists. There ain't one that ain't days away.

Young Bill (*rising*) White House made a special phone call.

Dennis the Whaler Son, even the President can't produce an icebreaker when there ain't one.

Young Bill President drew a blank. Right. No US ships.

Dennis the Whaler So – end of story.

Young Bill (*shaking his head*) No. Beginning of story, Dad. He made a second call.

Joe the Whaler What??? But there's no one. Godammit who Bill??? Who was the call to??

Music

Spotlight snaps on red flags high above the stage held by female Russian sailors in white. This is the crew of the Soviet icebreaker 'Admiral Makarov'. Immediate singing of The Internationale *in Russian.*

ИНТЕРНАЦИОНАЛ

Вставай проклятьем заклейменный,
Весь мир голодных и рабов!

Then, during the singing a loud cawing and the **Raven** *is revealed, among the Soviet sailors holding a red flag.*

Raven Cawwwwwwwwwwwwwwwwwwwwwwwwww.

The Internationale builds. During the singing the two surviving whales breach and breathe. Even higher than before. The Inuit cheer and throw their cutters into the air.

Кипит наш разум возмущенный
И в смертный бой идти готов.

Весь мир насилья мы разрушим
До основанья, а затем
Мы наш, мы новый мир построим –
Кто был ничем – тот станет всем.

Припев.
Это есть наш последний
И решительный бой!
С интернационалом
Воспрянет род людской.

Долго в цепях нас держали,
Долго нас голод томил.
Черные дни миновали,
Час искупленья пробил.

Свергнем могучей рукою
Гнет роковой навсегда!
И водрузим над Землею
Светлое знамя труда.

Припев.

(Internationale)

(Arise ye starvelings from your slumbers,
　　Arise ye criminals of want,
For reason in revolt now thunders,
　　And at last ends the age of cant.
Now away with all superstitions,
　　Servile masses, arise! arise!
We'll change forthwith the old conditions
　　And spurn the dust to win the prize.

(*Chorus:*)
Then comrades, come rally,
　　The last fight let us face –

The Internationale unites the human race.
 Then comrades, come rally,
 The last fight let us face –
The Internationale unites the human race.

No saviours from on high deliver,
 No trust have we in prince or peer;
Our own right hand the chains must shiver,
 Chains of hatred, of greed and fear.
Ere the thieves will disgorge their booty,
 And to all give a happier lot,
Each at his forge must do his duty
 And strike the iron when it's hot.)

(*Repeat Chorus.*)

The Internationale *swells to a conclusion as the front gauze falls. Lights fade. Continue cheering as – front gauze down.*

Interval.

Act Two

Scene One

Music begins.

Bring up light on stage and we see through front cloth the fog. Cloth taken out and fog covers the stage. In the fog we hear but don't see the whales breach and breathe. Weaker now. They dive.

Out of the fog comes **Sedna**. *Arctic sea birds come to her out of the fog – the creatures of her realm. She is friendly with them. Touches them. They fly off.*

Then music changes and through the fog at the opposite side of the stage comes the **Raven**. *His sound at low intense level.*

Raven Cawwwwwwwwwww!!

Sedna *and the* **Raven** *look across the stage at each other as the* **Storyteller** *enters.*

Raven Cawwwwwwwwwwwwwwwwww.

Storyteller 'Allow the humans to save these whales, Sedna!' cried the Raven. 'Comb your hair, free them and I promise to fly away and live in some other land. You will never see me again.'

Sedna (*a strong sound.*) Pijjaiunirmat. (Never.)

Storyteller 'Humans? Who cut my hands from me? Who plunder the sea and ice for oil and put all sea creatures in danger? Humans? Who still plunder the sea for the whales, the children of my thumb? Help THEM???;

Storyteller *starts to move into the fog.*

Sedna *holds up her bandaged bloody arms to the* **Raven**

Sedna Taimak tulugak. Taimak. (No Raven!! No more!!)

The words echo.

Raven (*defiantly*) Cawwwwwwwwwwwwwwwwwwwwwwwwwwwwwww.

This echoes. Then from behind them a great ripping of ice and creaking iron. The sound of the Soviet ice-breaker. **Sedna** *turns away into the fog. The sound of enthusiastic shouts from the ice-breaker – 'Admiral Makarov'.*

Voice Off Здравствуйте! Мы приехали! Советские моряки здесь. Хэлло! Хэлло!
(Hello. We're here. The Russians are here. Hello.)

*The **Raven** caws in expectation of success.*

Raven Caaaawwwwwwww!!

*The **Raven** exits into the fog.*

Scene Two

*Then enter through the thinning fog two female Russian sailors with Soviet flag. These are the **Captain** of the Soviet icebreaker 'Admiral Makarov' and the ship's **2nd officer**.*

Then enter from another direction Minneapolis Dad *and his mate* **Ricky** *with the stars and stripes.*

Then entering from a third direction – two Inuit: **Joe** *and* **Dennis**. *They stand watching the meeting.*

Soviet Ship Captain (*as they approach*) American!!

Minneapolis Dad Russki! *Perestroika!*

Soviet Ship Captain (*pointing at American, friendly*) Perry Mason! I – from Georgia.

Minneapolis Dad What? I born in Georgia. Atlanta.

Soviet Ship Captain Tibilisi. (*Singing as Ray Charles song.*) Georgia. Georgia.

They laugh and hug. As they do so flags are planted in the ice.

Soviet 2nd Officer She Captain. Ice break ship. No good English her.

Minneapolis Dad (*disagreeing and still close to Soviet Ship **Captain***) Fantastic English. (*As Ray Charles.*) Georgia.

Soviet Ship Captain (*as Ray Charles*) Georgia.

Minneapolis Dad (*turns to introduce the Inuit to the Russians*) Inuit. American citizens. Very good.

Ricky Cut ice holes for two weeks. Many. Tired now. But save whales. Very good.

Soviet 2nd Officer Inuit? Russia too live Inuit. (*Indicating his*

Captain.) Her. Mother. Inuit of Siberia.

Joe the Whaler (*delighted to make this discovery. To Second Inuit.*) Her. Russian Inuit.

Dennis the Whaler Aghhhhhhhh. Inuit!!

And they both clasp the Russian **Captain** *in turn.*

Soviet Ship Captain (*offering*) Vodka!! Cold.

Minneapolis Dad (*accepting*) Thanks, Skipper. Very cold.

Soviet Ship Captain Skipper, Haha. Skipper. (*Toasts.*) Whales. Before, Soviet kill whales. Many. Big many. No more.

Soviet 2nd Officer Last year we save 70 Beluga. Yes. White whale. Beautiful. 70. Crash ice. 'Go home Beluga.' Beautiful.

Ricky One hundred and forty years ago American whaling captain discovered Grey whales. Captain Charles Scamman. Kill nearly all. Harpoon. Now we kill – no more.

All (*toasting*) No more!

Ricky Only Inuit can kill whale here now. One or two because they have always been hunters. And now they help Siku and Putu.

Soviet Ship Captain Siku, Putu good?

Ricky (*demonstrating*) Not too good. Jagged ice in breathing holes. Hurt heads. Blood. Not so strong now.

Sound of helicopter.

Minneapolis Dad Not again!! (*To Russians.*) TV. Newspapers.

Soviet 2nd Officer (*to* **Captain**) Телевидение. Газеты. (TV. Newspapers.)

Soviet Ship Captain Ah. New York Times. NBC.

Ricky Toronto Star. El Pais. London Daily Mail. Corriere de la Sera. You can't move around here.

A rope ladder falls from the top.

Minneapolis Dad Hey, you guys. These whales are in bad shape now. Media Whirlibirds comin' over on the hour every hour they don't need. So – last picture.

This as a **Photographer** *has come down a few feet on the rope ladder so he can be seen by everyone.*

Photographer Hey guys, these whales belong to the world now. This is the front page. Not Madonna. Not Nancy. These.

Ricky Listen pal. When you press guys start cutting ice like these Inuit been doing for two weeks straight – at night, all night – then you can call the shots. Photo finito – comprende?

Photographer OKKKKKKKKK. OK buddy. But hey, Russians and Americans working together? That hasn't happened since the war. So ya wanna do the hug one more time? *Glasnost* right. Mickey Mouse and the Bear.

They nod and clasp and pose. All looking up at the camera.

Soviet Ship Captain Vodka.

Minneapolis Dad Coca Cola.

Ricky Cheese.

Soviet Ship Captain Cheese?

Soviet 2nd Officer (*explaining*) Улыбайтесь, пожалуйста! (Smile, please.)

Soviet Ship Captain Ahhh!!

All Cheese.

Photographer Thanks guys. All the best. Set them free.

And he is starting to be pulled up on the rope as the helicopter noise continues.

Soviet Ship Captain Putu? Siku?

Joe *gets out a large map and starts to unfold.*

Minneapolis Dad Behind us. We're keeping away. Give them a bit of peace.

Soviet 2nd Officer (**Captain**) Они – за нами. (They're behind us.)

Soviet Ship Captain Скажите американцам о наших спецификациях. (Tell the Americans our specifications.)

Soviet 2nd Officer OK. Strategic. The Captain say you we rip any ice you got so long as we got six metres water under ship.

Joe the Whaler *has now spread the map. Map is like an Inuit painting. It shows: the outline of the coast including the Inuit settlement with pictures of the Inuit; the original holes where the whales were found; ice* *holes leading from there towards the sea; the pack ice and sea channels beyond the ice; in the pack ice the Russian ship; the whales in the furthest ice hole to seaward; polar bears on other patches of ice; a helicopter above the whales. With photographers; Inuit cutting the new ice holes.*

Joe the Whaler (*swiftly through map*) Whales originally I find here. (*Indicating where.*) Inuit been cutting new ice holes for two weeks. Edge of the ice two weeks ago was here. Temperature's dropped 20 degrees and now ice this far out and moving fast.

Simultaneous quiet translation to the Soviet **Captain**.

Soviet 2nd Officer No problem

Dennis the Whaler (*indicating*) OK we think it's deep water in as far as here. Start smashing the channel soon as you like. It'll bring you to within thousand metres of the whales. While you're crushing ice we'll cut new ice holes and come towards you. Here, here, here, and so on.

Soviet 2nd Officer When Siku, Putu reach open sea? Good chance?

Ricky (*indicating on map*) Latest satellite pictures show there are leads for them to swim in all through the Chukchi sea. They've got every chance of spending Christmas off Mexico.

Soviet Ship Captain *has been nodding through this. She's understood it all.*

Soviet Ship Captain (*to the whales*) Merry Christmas ladies.

Minneapolis Dad Thanks fellas!!

And the map is folded as –

Soviet Ship Captain Давайте растопим эту глыбу льда! (OK let's cut goddamn ice!)

Minneapolis Dad What did the Captain say?

Soviet 2nd Officer Captain say. 'Let's cut some goddamn ice!'

The Americans and the Inuit laugh.

Minneapolis Dad Hey tell her she sounds just like John Wayne.

Soviet Ship Captain John Wayne? Hey. The Duke. Red River.

They laughingly tap each other. Another distant helicopter sound.

Minneapolis Dad Jeeez!!! More TV. What's happening?

Soviet 2nd Officer Our town – Vladivostock. We hear about whales Moscow Radio. All the kids. 'Save Siku. Save Putu.' All the time. 'Siku. Putu.'

Minneapolis Dad Seems like humans are ready to listen to the whales now instead of harpooning them.

Ricky Yea? Tell Japan. They ain't listening to nobody.

Soviet Ship Captain (*in English like John Wayne*) Let's cut some goddamn ice!

And starts to walk off with John Wayne sideways walk. They laugh and exit as helicopter noise comes up.

Scene Three

A rope ladder descends. An Australian radio woman starts coming down the ladder doing her first radio piece on North Slope. Bush hat etc. Not dressed for the climate.

Aussie Journo Station 2 Triple Z. Sydney, Australia. North Slope, Alaska. (*Cold.*) Cripes!! In the distance I can see the Russian boat – the 'Admiral Makarov' starting very slowly from the open sea to crack a great mountain of ice that must be in the way of the whales' escape. Working towards them cutting holes in the ice are gangs of men. Must be Inuit I reckon but they don't look like I seen on the old movies. And I don't see igloos either. Must be somewhere else. Hey but there are some of the local kids running towards the helicopter. Reckon it must be for some traditional Inuit greeting. They won't undersand it but I'll give them the traditional Aussie greeting.

She is near or at the bottom of the ladder. The Inuit kids enter.

Aussie Journo G'day kids.

First Inuit Kid Hey look. Crocodile Dundee's sister!! G'day.

Others Yea!! G'day.

Aussie Journo You've heard of Croc –???

Second Inuit Kid Sure. Video. You know Paul Hogan?

Third Inuit Kid When's Crocodile Dundee 3 coming out?

Aussie Journo Hotel. You know what a hotel is?

Third Inuit Kid Hotel's full. But my Mum's got a room.

Aussie Journo I'll take it. I read you take payment in stones or somethin'?

Third Inuit Kid Two hundred dollars a night.

Aussie Journo What??? Two hundred – What?

Inuit kids look offstage.

Third Inuit Kid Hey there's another Canadian TV crew landing.

It looks as if they are about to move off in search of more profitable pickings.

Aussie Journo I'll take the room!

Fourth Inuit Kid Need someone to take you to the whales?

Aussie Journo No. Yes. Yes. How long before they're free?

Fourth Inuit Kid Our Dads are gonna free the whales by tonight. But you're gonna need a snow mobile or you won't see anything. My big brother's got one.

Aussie Journo Yea. Yea. Yea. How much?

Fourth Inuit Kid Two hundred a day.

First Inuit Kid My sister charged TV Italy three hundred.

Aussie Journo Two hundred. Oh cripes. I'll take it.

Second Inuit Kid You hungry Miss?

Aussie Journo I'm starving. Hey but –

Second Inuit Kid The only restaurant's booked out. Ya want to eat at my sister's hut?

Aussie Journo Do I have any choice? How much?

Second Inuit Kid Twenty dollars a plate.

Aussie Journo OK. OK. Is it traditional Inuit cooking?

Second Inuit Kid Yea. Inuit Hamburgers.

Aussie Journo (*to the heavens*) Get me out of here! No take me to the whales. I got to send a story back to Oz.

She then starts to move off.

First Inuit Kid How ya wanna pay? You on an expense account Lady?

Aussie Journo Company cheque OK? You wouldn't have heard of him but I work for a Rupert Murdoch station.

All (*to each other whispering*) Murdoch!!!

Second Inuit Kid (*to another whispering*) Twentieth-Century Fox. Sky TV.

First Inuit Kid (*to another whispering*) Nuts. We shoulda doubled the price!

Aussie Journo Or I got American Express.

All Kids (*as they take the card*) American Express? (*A beat. As if they've never heard of it.*) That'll do nicely!!!!

They exit. Music. Lights down.

Scene Four

On the ice. Sound of Arctic wind. Empty stage with two ice holes. One near front stage and one much further back.

Enter **Minneapolis Dad** *and the* **Soviet 2nd Officer**. *They look in the back hole. Then they come forward to the hole at the front of the stage.*

Minneapolis Dad (*looking out front. The direction of the open sea*) Maybe Siku and Putu already moved to one of the new holes we cut.

Soviet 2nd Officer All they need now swim under ice – hole to hole – and they got deep channel waiting them.

Minneapolis Dad They'd be dead without your icebreaker Russki. Dead and buried.

Soviet 2nd Officer Which hole Putu, Siku in last night?

Minneapolis Dad (*indicating the one behind*) That.

Soviet 2nd Officer OK you me check each hole towards sea.

Minneapolis Dad (*hearing something behind him*) What's that?

Soviet 2nd Officer No!

Sound begins to happen to the back of them. The sound of the whales about to breach.

Minneapolis Dad They've come back to the same hole!!! Don't they want to get out of here?

And the whales breach in the back breathing hole.

Both Noooooooooooooo.

Soviet 2nd Officer (*going towards back hole*) Siku. Putu. You know what out there? Freedom. Why you not want go there dumdums!?

Minneapolis Dad Maybe they got too used to being round humans.

Soviet 2nd Officer Go! Go! Go! You die here.

Minneapolis Dad Shoot!!

*Then the second American **Ricky** enters.*

Minneapolis Dad Bad news here Ricky.

Ricky I know. Found 'em an hour ago. But don't worry. Had a great idea to move 'em.

Soviet 2nd Officer What?

Ricky What'd make you move fast?

Minneapolis Dad Shark'd do a pretty good job.

Ricky Close. (*Into radio.*) OK Control, play the tape when you're ready and big volume.

Soviet 2nd Officer What is?

Ricky Public enemy No 1 for the Californian Grey.

And straightaway and very loud the sound of killer whales.

Ricky Killer whales. This'll get 'em to the sea and pronto.

They stand by the front hole to which the whales should be moving.

All Come on. Come on. Come on.

Ricky Don't you hear them?? These're the guys that can tear your heads off!!

Soviet 2nd Officer Dumdum whales! Move out!!

Minneapolis Dad What's wrong with them? Don't you know who that is??

Ricky (*into radio*) OK. Turn it off. No reaction.

The sound ceases. They stand there and look at the whales still in the holes. Then at the back **Joe the Whaler** *comes on. He has a stick with him.* **Joe** *goes to the ice hole. He kneels down. They turn to look.*

Minneapolis Dad Joe?

Joe *puts hands to his lips. Talks to the whales and then stands and taps one of them on the head. A loud noise and the whales dive. Music.*

Ricky (*with a sense of excitement and possible success*) What's happening?

Joe *moves forward slowly to the second hole looking down at the ice. He joins the others at the forward (seaward) hole. The sound of the whales approaching. They breach and breathe. All cheer.*

Minneapolis Dad Joe, tell 'em to do the same for ten more holes and they're looking straight at Mexico.

Joe *nods. He taps the head of the whales again. They stay there.*

Soviet 2nd Officer Again. Siku. Putu. Come ladies. Please. Joe, again.

Joe *taps them again and walks away across front stage. He looks back. The whales stay there.*

Minneapolis Dad Joe, how about we leave them to you? Maybe they don't want us here right now. And Joe, tell 'em every hour they wait those sea channels the Russkis are making are icing back over.

They nod and go. They don't look hopeful now. **Joe** *looks down at the whales.*

Joe the Whaler Why won't you go? There is something we're doing wrong here but I don't know what.

An **Old Inuit Woman** *has entered.*

Joe the Whaler Grandmother you seen the whale hunt all your life. They won't move. What are we doing wrong here? We're running out of time.

Old Inuit Those the holes you cut up ahead?

Joe the Whaler Yes. Big holes.

Old Inuit How deep's the water under those holes?

Joe the Whaler OK there's deeper water other directions, Grandmother, but we got a problem. We gotta avoid that great mountain of ice up ahead. Our holes only three, four metres maybe to the sea bed.

Old Inuit Grandson if you want to save these you'd better start thinking like a whale.

*The **Raven** has entered and listens.*

Joe the Whaler OK. Tell me how.

Old Inuit What's that whale thinking? She's thinking – there's holes in front of me and yea, they're in the direction I got to migrate. Good. But the water's shallow. My head's telling me that. Could get stuck. Could get stuck below the ice and drown. Hey. What about staying where I am? Least there's a hole here. Least I can breathe. And the water's deep. And there's these dumb Inuit sweating for weeks cutting ice for me. Boy I ain't seen that before. Yea. All things considered I'll stay here.

Joe the Whaler But they'll die.

Old Inuit She's confused. She thinks you're gonna go on cutting. She don't know in a few days ice'll be so thick you won't be able to cut it. See, youngster, she don't know what November in Alaska is like. No Grey whale ever saw it. They gone south by October or they don't live to pass on the news.

Joe the Whaler So what are you saying Grandmother?

Old Inuit I'm saying you got a problem. Seems like Sedna's unhappy again and her hair's maybe gonna drown them. If that's so there's nothing humans can do about it. (*A beat.*) One human maybe could have but he's long dead and in the ground in California. (*She rises.*) Only one thing you can do, youngster. Eat them.

*The **Old Inuit** goes. **Joe the Whaler** takes a last look at the whales. He shakes his head. **Joe the Whaler** leaves. Music change. Slowly and from several directions a number of polar bears approach the holes. The **Raven** watches and defends.*

Raven Cawwwww.

The whales breach and disappear. The bears get closer to the holes and their kill.

Raven Caaaaaaaaawwwwwwwwwwwwwwwwwwwww!!!!

*The bears roar in return. And with a mighty series of croaks the **Raven** does a Bruce Lee on the bears. They retreat. But clearly not for ever. Still* *roaring at the* **Raven**. *As lights fade on the frustrated* **Raven**. *What to do?*

Raven Cawwwwwwwwwwwwwwwwwwwww.

Scene Five

A graveyard in San Francisco, California. Perhaps only a single gravestone.

A small group of tourists enter preceded by a **Tour Guide** *with a megaphone.*

Tour Guide Ladies and gentlemen for the last part of our tour of California – the San Francisco Cemetery. The graves of politicians, film stars, and sailors.

The tourists wander around taking pictures etc.

Tour Guide Of special interest today, I guess, as world interest centres on Putu and Siku, is the grave of the whaling Captain who first discovered the Grey whale off this coast in 1846. Charles Scamman.

Raven *enters.*

Tour Guide From 1846 until the dawn of this century his whaling ships followed the Greys from their winter feeding grounds in Alaska down to Mexico and back again. Killing whales in thousands.

Raven *squawks angrily at the tourists.*

Raven Caaawwwwwww.

Raven *knocks on the gravestone as the tourists move back a few steps.*

Tour Guide ((*nervous of* **Raven**) Ahem. But in the process Captain Scamman came to know more about the Grey Whale than any man has ever done. Perhaps if he were alive he could save –

Raven Cawwwwwwwwwwwww!!!!!!!

This frightens the tourists. They start to run.

Tour Guide Back to the bus folks!!!! This here bird seems a little frisky. (*To* **Raven**.) Easy Mac!! Easy!!

Raven *knocks again hard on the gravestone.* **Raven** *caws again at the tourists and frightens the last ones away. Music change.*

The earth starts to move under the gravestone. A hand comes up and then a second holding a bloody wooden harpoon. Then the earth falls back and man in a top hat and nineteenth-century sea clothes rises through the earth. The spirit of the American whaling **Captain Scamman** *stands. He holds the bloody harpoon.*

Raven Caaaaaaaaaaaawwwwwwwwwwwww.

Captain Scamman Putu? Siku?

The **Raven** *affirms that is the point of his visit.*

Captain Scamman Raven, do you come to mock us, the ghosts of old harpooners who walk these Californian beaches?

Raven Cawwww.

Captain Scamman And what we are obliged to look upon? Where once the pods of Grey whales took days and days to pass as they swam between Alaska and Mexico in their hundreds of thousands now we poor ghosts watch ones and twos, small families and know it was we who hunted them to the very edge of extinction. Never thinking. Never asking – where will the killing lead?

Raven (*agitated*) Caaawwwww.

Captain Scamman Too late Raven! They are tangled in Sedna's hair. Perhaps she wishes to save them from the harpooners of Japan who still wait; who still slaughter. And who can blame her wanting to keep her children with her after what we have done!!

Raven Cawwwwwwwwww.

Raven *insistently grabs the* **Captain.**

Captain Scamman It's too late Raven.

Raven Cawwwwwwwwwwwwwww.

And **Captain Scamman** *takes hold of the* **Raven***. Music.* **Raven** *and the* **Captain** *are whipped into the air. They fly.*

Scene Six

Raven *and* **Captain Scamman** *are flying high above the stage as the* **Storyteller** *enters.*

Raven Caaaaaaaaaaaaaaaaawwwwwwwwwwwwwwwwwwwwwwwwww.

Storyteller North along the coast of California they flew. Oregon coast now. Following the migration route of the Grey whale. The coast of Washington State and colder now. Across the border of Canada and ever northwards. A journey Captain Scamman had taken so many, many times to kill the Grey whale. Now he would give anything to save them but how? How?

Raven Caaaaaaaawwwwwwwwww.

Storyteller Cried the sad raven when he looked down on the frozen North Coast of Alaska, on Siku and Putu and their poor blood covered heads. Saw how Sedna had allowed the wind and the frozen sea to make another mountain of ice to block the whales' pathway to the sea. He looked down and saw the Russian ship helpless and the Inuit throw down their ice cutting knives in despair.

Raven Caaaaaaaaaaaaaawwwwwwwwwwwwwwwwwwww.

Storyteller 'Sedna cannot forget the loss of her hands and the ruin of her hair. The whales will die. I know it now.' The Raven looked down into the icy waters and he saw the polar bears.

Polar bears enter.

Storyteller Saw arctic fish. The elephant seals. The Bowhead whale.

These animals have entered. **Sedna** *enters with bandaged hands. She is the focal point of the dance.*

Storyteller And far far below the surface he saw Sedna with her poor tangled neglected hair.

Raven Caaaaaaaaaaaaaaaaaaawwwwwwww.

The dance continues.

Storyteller And Sedna looked up through the icy water, saw the Raven and then saw the famous whaling Captain who had killed so many of her children. (*A beat.*) And saw that he would save Siku and Putu if he could. Might the whites change that much?

Sedna Tamaanipit Scamman? (Scamman is it you?)

Captain Scamman Yes it is I, Sedna.

Storyteller And Captain Scamman reached into his pocket and brought out something which he had made so many years ago from the tooth of a whale. It was a comb.

Captain Scamman Quickly Raven, show Sedna you love her. You always have.

Raven Caaaaaaaaawwwwwwwwwwww.

And the **Raven** *descends into the sea with the comb while* **Captain Scamman** *flies above them.* **Sedna** *turns and looks at him. The* **Raven** *holds up the comb to find out if this offer will be accepted.*

Storyteller Sedna turned from the Raven and saw above her the trapped whales still bravely struggling to reach the air, struggling to live. But very weak now. Saw Captain Scamman waiting, waiting. Hoping. Hoping. Could she forgive the Raven and man and let the whales swim for Mexico?

A pause and then **Sedna** *turns to the* **Raven** *and nods. Music.* **Raven** *starts to gently comb her hair. With her hair still being combed we hear the whales being released from her hair and the ice walls crashing. The dancers swirl in time with the continuing sound over which the sounds of home going whales are prominent. Music has changed to a Mexican theme, a trumpet and guitar led band. Mixed with whale sounds. Dancing continues. Fog representing the breaking ice comes down starting to mask the dancers.*

Front gauze comes down. On the gauze, giant colour underwater film footage of Grey whales in tropical water swimming vigorously as the dance continues to the sounds of Mexico. The lights on the dancers fade leaving only the photography of the whales. Then lights come up on the cast so that their wave and bow to the audience is done with the whales still swimming and sounding.